MW01097488

RECIPES

Delica Publications

# MEASUREMENTS

| CUP | TBSP | TSP |
|---|---|---|
| 1/16 | 1 | 3 |
| 1/8 | 2 | 6 |
| 1/4 | 4 | 12 |
| 1/3 | 5⅓ | 16 |
| 1/2 | 8 | 24 |
| 2/3 | 10⅔ | 32 |
| 3/4 | 12 | 36 |
| 1 | 16 | 28 |

| OVEN TEMPERATURES | |
|---|---|
| 140° C | 275° F |
| 150° C | 300° F |
| 165° C | 325° F |
| 177° C | 350° F |
| 190° C | 375° F |
| 200° C | 400° F |
| 220° C | 425° F |
| 230° C | 450° F |

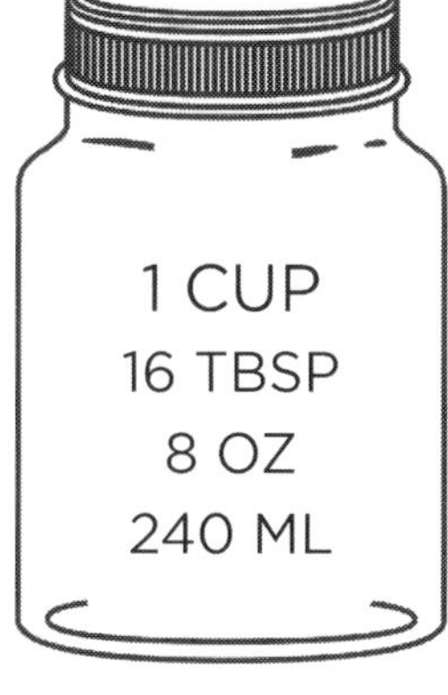


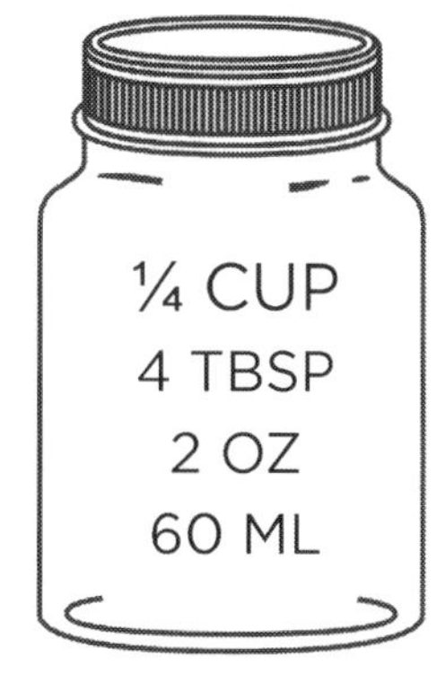

| OUNCES | ½ | 1 | 2 | 3 | 4 | 5 | 8 | 10 | 16 |
|---|---|---|---|---|---|---|---|---|---|
| GRAMS | 14 | 28 | 57 | 85 | 113 | 142 | 227 | 284 | 454 |

# TABLE OF CONTENTS

| # | RECIPE | MEAL TYPE |
|---|---|---|
| 1 | | |
| 2 | | |
| 3 | | |
| 4 | | |
| 5 | | |
| 6 | | |
| 7 | | |
| 8 | | |
| 9 | | |
| 10 | | |
| 11 | | |
| 12 | | |
| 13 | | |
| 14 | | |
| 15 | | |
| 16 | | |
| 17 | | |
| 18 | | |
| 19 | | |
| 20 | | |
| 21 | | |
| 22 | | |
| 23 | | |
| 24 | | |
| 25 | | |
| 26 | | |
| 27 | | |
| 28 | | |
| 29 | | |
| 30 | | |
| 31 | | |
| 32 | | |
| 33 | | |

# TABLE OF CONTENTS

# TABLE OF CONTENTS

# RECIPE : 1

PREP TIME

COOK TIME

SERVES

MEAL TYPE

INGREDIENTS :

INSTRUCTIONS :

NOTES :

# RECIPE : 2

PREP TIME

COOK TIME

SERVES

MEAL TYPE

INGREDIENTS :

INSTRUCTIONS :

NOTES :

# RECIPE : 3

PREP TIME

COOK TIME

SERVES

MEAL TYPE

INGREDIENTS :

INSTRUCTIONS :

NOTES :

# RECIPE : 4

PREP TIME

COOK TIME

SERVES

MEAL TYPE

INGREDIENTS :

INSTRUCTIONS :

NOTES :

# RECIPE : 5

PREP TIME

COOK TIME

SERVES

MEAL TYPE

INGREDIENTS :

INSTRUCTIONS :

NOTES :

# RECIPE : 6

PREP TIME

COOK TIME

SERVES

MEAL TYPE

INGREDIENTS :

INSTRUCTIONS :

NOTES :

# RECIPE : 7

PREP TIME

COOK TIME

SERVES

MEAL TYPE

INGREDIENTS :

INSTRUCTIONS :

NOTES :

# RECIPE : 8

PREP TIME

COOK TIME

SERVES

MEAL TYPE

INGREDIENTS :

INSTRUCTIONS :

NOTES :

# RECIPE : 9

PREP TIME

COOK TIME

SERVES

MEAL TYPE

INGREDIENTS :

INSTRUCTIONS :

NOTES :

# RECIPE : 10

PREP TIME

COOK TIME

SERVES

MEAL TYPE

INGREDIENTS :

INSTRUCTIONS :

NOTES :

# RECIPE : 11

PREP TIME

COOK TIME

SERVES

MEAL TYPE

INGREDIENTS :

INSTRUCTIONS :

NOTES :

# RECIPE : 12

PREP TIME

COOK TIME

SERVES

MEAL TYPE

INGREDIENTS :

INSTRUCTIONS :

NOTES :

# RECIPE : 13

PREP TIME

COOK TIME

SERVES

MEAL TYPE

INGREDIENTS :

-
-
-
-
-
-
-
-
-
-
-
-
-
-
-
-
-
-

INSTRUCTIONS :

NOTES :

# RECIPE : 14

PREP TIME

COOK TIME

SERVES

MEAL TYPE

INGREDIENTS :

INSTRUCTIONS :

NOTES :

# RECIPE : 15

PREP TIME

COOK TIME

SERVES

MEAL TYPE

INGREDIENTS :

- 
- 
- 
- 
- 
- 
- 
- 
- 
- 
- 
- 
- 
- 
- 
- 
- 
- 

INSTRUCTIONS :

NOTES :

# RECIPE : 16

PREP TIME

COOK TIME

SERVES

MEAL TYPE

INGREDIENTS :

INSTRUCTIONS :

NOTES :

# RECIPE : 17

PREP TIME

COOK TIME

SERVES

MEAL TYPE

INGREDIENTS :

INSTRUCTIONS :

NOTES :

# RECIPE : 18

PREP TIME

COOK TIME

SERVES

MEAL TYPE

INGREDIENTS :

- 
- 
- 
- 
- 
- 
- 
- 
- 
- 
- 
- 
- 
- 
- 
- 
- 
- 

INSTRUCTIONS :

NOTES :

# RECIPE : 19

PREP TIME

COOK TIME

SERVES

MEAL TYPE

INGREDIENTS :

INSTRUCTIONS :

NOTES :

# RECIPE : 20

PREP TIME

COOK TIME

SERVES

MEAL TYPE

INGREDIENTS :

INSTRUCTIONS :

NOTES :

# RECIPE : 21

PREP TIME

COOK TIME

SERVES

MEAL TYPE

INGREDIENTS :

INSTRUCTIONS :

NOTES :

# RECIPE : 22

PREP TIME

COOK TIME

SERVES

MEAL TYPE

INGREDIENTS :

INSTRUCTIONS :

NOTES :

# RECIPE : 23

PREP TIME

COOK TIME

SERVES

MEAL TYPE

INGREDIENTS :

INSTRUCTIONS :

NOTES :

# RECIPE : 24

PREP TIME

COOK TIME

SERVES

MEAL TYPE

INGREDIENTS :

INSTRUCTIONS :

NOTES :

# RECIPE : 25

PREP TIME

COOK TIME

SERVES

MEAL TYPE

INGREDIENTS :

•
•
•
•
•
•
•
•
•
•
•
•
•
•
•
•
•
•

INSTRUCTIONS :

NOTES :

# RECIPE : 26

PREP TIME

COOK TIME

SERVES

MEAL TYPE

INGREDIENTS :

INSTRUCTIONS :

NOTES :

# RECIPE : 27

PREP TIME

COOK TIME

SERVES

MEAL TYPE

INGREDIENTS :

INSTRUCTIONS :

NOTES :

# RECIPE : 28

PREP TIME

COOK TIME

SERVES

MEAL TYPE

INGREDIENTS :

INSTRUCTIONS :

NOTES :

# RECIPE : 29

PREP TIME

COOK TIME

SERVES

MEAL TYPE

INGREDIENTS :

INSTRUCTIONS :

NOTES :

# RECIPE : 30

PREP TIME

COOK TIME

SERVES

MEAL TYPE

INGREDIENTS :

INSTRUCTIONS :

NOTES :

# RECIPE : 31

PREP TIME

COOK TIME

SERVES

MEAL TYPE

INGREDIENTS :

INSTRUCTIONS :

NOTES :

# RECIPE : 32

PREP TIME

COOK TIME

SERVES

MEAL TYPE

INGREDIENTS :

INSTRUCTIONS :

NOTES :

# RECIPE : 33

PREP TIME

COOK TIME

SERVES

MEAL TYPE

INGREDIENTS :

INSTRUCTIONS :

NOTES :

# RECIPE : 34

PREP TIME

COOK TIME

SERVES

MEAL TYPE

INGREDIENTS :

INSTRUCTIONS :

NOTES :

# RECIPE : 35

PREP TIME

COOK TIME

SERVES

MEAL TYPE

INGREDIENTS :

INSTRUCTIONS :

NOTES :

# RECIPE : 36

PREP TIME

COOK TIME

SERVES

MEAL TYPE

INGREDIENTS :

INSTRUCTIONS :

NOTES :

# RECIPE : 37

PREP TIME

COOK TIME

SERVES

MEAL TYPE

INGREDIENTS :

•
•
•
•
•
•
•
•
•
•
•
•
•
•
•
•
•
•

INSTRUCTIONS :

NOTES :

# RECIPE : 38

PREP TIME

COOK TIME

SERVES

MEAL TYPE

INGREDIENTS :

INSTRUCTIONS :

NOTES :

# RECIPE : 39

PREP TIME

COOK TIME

SERVES

MEAL TYPE

INGREDIENTS :

INSTRUCTIONS :

NOTES :

# RECIPE : 40

PREP TIME

COOK TIME

SERVES

MEAL TYPE

INGREDIENTS :

INSTRUCTIONS :

NOTES :

# RECIPE : 41

PREP TIME

COOK TIME

SERVES

MEAL TYPE

INGREDIENTS :

INSTRUCTIONS :

NOTES :

# RECIPE : 42

PREP TIME

COOK TIME

SERVES

MEAL TYPE

INGREDIENTS :

-
-
-
-
-
-
-
-
-
-
-
-
-
-
-
-
-
-

INSTRUCTIONS :

NOTES :

# RECIPE : 43

PREP TIME

COOK TIME

SERVES

MEAL TYPE

INGREDIENTS :

INSTRUCTIONS :

NOTES :

# RECIPE : 44

PREP TIME

COOK TIME

SERVES

MEAL TYPE

INGREDIENTS :

INSTRUCTIONS :

NOTES :

# RECIPE : 45

PREP TIME

COOK TIME

SERVES

MEAL TYPE

INGREDIENTS :

INSTRUCTIONS :

NOTES :

# RECIPE : 46

PREP TIME

COOK TIME

SERVES

MEAL TYPE

INGREDIENTS :

INSTRUCTIONS :

NOTES :

# RECIPE : 47

PREP TIME

COOK TIME

SERVES

MEAL TYPE

INGREDIENTS :

INSTRUCTIONS :

NOTES :

# RECIPE : 48

PREP TIME

COOK TIME

SERVES

MEAL TYPE

INGREDIENTS :

INSTRUCTIONS :

NOTES :

# RECIPE : 49

PREP TIME

COOK TIME

SERVES

MEAL TYPE

INGREDIENTS :

INSTRUCTIONS :

NOTES :

# RECIPE : 50

PREP TIME

COOK TIME

SERVES

MEAL TYPE

INGREDIENTS :

INSTRUCTIONS :

NOTES :

# RECIPE : 51

PREP TIME

COOK TIME

SERVES

MEAL TYPE

INGREDIENTS :

INSTRUCTIONS :

NOTES :

# RECIPE : 52

PREP TIME

COOK TIME

SERVES

MEAL TYPE

INGREDIENTS :

INSTRUCTIONS :

NOTES :

# RECIPE : 53

PREP TIME

COOK TIME

SERVES

MEAL TYPE

INGREDIENTS :

- 
- 
- 
- 
- 
- 
- 
- 
- 
- 
- 
- 
- 
- 
- 
- 
- 
- 

INSTRUCTIONS :

NOTES :

# RECIPE : 54

PREP TIME

COOK TIME

SERVES

MEAL TYPE

INGREDIENTS :

- 
- 
- 
- 
- 
- 
- 
- 
- 
- 
- 
- 
- 
- 
- 
- 
- 
- 

INSTRUCTIONS :

NOTES :

# RECIPE : 55

PREP TIME

COOK TIME

SERVES

MEAL TYPE

INGREDIENTS :

INSTRUCTIONS :

NOTES :

# RECIPE : 56

PREP TIME

COOK TIME

SERVES

MEAL TYPE

INGREDIENTS :

INSTRUCTIONS :

NOTES :

# RECIPE : 57

PREP TIME

COOK TIME

SERVES

MEAL TYPE

INGREDIENTS :

INSTRUCTIONS :

NOTES :

# RECIPE : 58

PREP TIME

COOK TIME

SERVES

MEAL TYPE

INGREDIENTS :

INSTRUCTIONS :

NOTES :

# RECIPE : 59

PREP TIME

COOK TIME

SERVES

MEAL TYPE

INGREDIENTS :

INSTRUCTIONS :

NOTES :

# RECIPE : 60

PREP TIME

COOK TIME

SERVES

MEAL TYPE

INGREDIENTS :

INSTRUCTIONS :

NOTES :

# RECIPE : 61

PREP TIME

COOK TIME

SERVES

MEAL TYPE

INGREDIENTS :

INSTRUCTIONS :

NOTES :

# RECIPE : 62

PREP TIME

COOK TIME

SERVES

MEAL TYPE

INGREDIENTS :

INSTRUCTIONS :

NOTES :

# RECIPE : 63

PREP TIME

COOK TIME

SERVES

MEAL TYPE

INGREDIENTS :

INSTRUCTIONS :

NOTES :

# RECIPE : 64

PREP TIME

COOK TIME

SERVES

MEAL TYPE

INGREDIENTS :

•
•
•
•
•
•
•
•
•
•
•
•
•
•
•
•
•
•

INSTRUCTIONS :

NOTES :

# RECIPE : 65

PREP TIME

COOK TIME

SERVES

MEAL TYPE

INGREDIENTS :

- 
- 
- 
- 
- 
- 
- 
- 
- 
- 
- 
- 
- 
- 
- 
- 
- 
- 

INSTRUCTIONS :

NOTES :

# RECIPE : 66

PREP TIME

COOK TIME

SERVES

MEAL TYPE

INGREDIENTS :

INSTRUCTIONS :

NOTES :

# RECIPE : 67

PREP TIME

COOK TIME

SERVES

MEAL TYPE

INGREDIENTS :

- 
- 
- 
- 
- 
- 
- 
- 
- 
- 
- 
- 
- 
- 
- 
- 
- 
- 

INSTRUCTIONS :

NOTES :

# RECIPE : 68

PREP TIME

COOK TIME

SERVES

MEAL TYPE

INGREDIENTS :

INSTRUCTIONS :

NOTES :

# RECIPE : 69

PREP TIME

COOK TIME

SERVES

MEAL TYPE

INGREDIENTS :

INSTRUCTIONS :

NOTES :

# RECIPE : 70

PREP TIME

COOK TIME

SERVES

MEAL TYPE

INGREDIENTS :

•
•
•
•
•
•
•
•
•
•
•
•
•
•
•
•
•
•

INSTRUCTIONS :

NOTES :

# RECIPE : 71

PREP TIME

COOK TIME

SERVES

MEAL TYPE

INGREDIENTS :

INSTRUCTIONS :

NOTES :

# RECIPE : 72

PREP TIME

COOK TIME

SERVES

MEAL TYPE

INGREDIENTS :

INSTRUCTIONS :

NOTES :

# RECIPE : 73

PREP TIME

COOK TIME

SERVES

MEAL TYPE

INGREDIENTS :

INSTRUCTIONS :

NOTES :

# RECIPE : 74

PREP TIME

COOK TIME

SERVES

MEAL TYPE

INGREDIENTS :

INSTRUCTIONS :

NOTES :

# RECIPE : 75

PREP TIME

COOK TIME

SERVES

MEAL TYPE

INGREDIENTS :

- 
- 
- 
- 
- 
- 
- 
- 
- 
- 
- 
- 
- 
- 
- 
- 
- 

INSTRUCTIONS :

NOTES :

# RECIPE : 76

PREP TIME

COOK TIME

SERVES

MEAL TYPE

INGREDIENTS :

INSTRUCTIONS :

NOTES :

# RECIPE : 77

PREP TIME

COOK TIME

SERVES

MEAL TYPE

INGREDIENTS :

INSTRUCTIONS :

NOTES :

# RECIPE : 78

PREP TIME

COOK TIME

SERVES

MEAL TYPE

INGREDIENTS :

INSTRUCTIONS :

NOTES :

# RECIPE : 79

PREP TIME

COOK TIME

SERVES

MEAL TYPE

INGREDIENTS :

INSTRUCTIONS :

NOTES :

# RECIPE : 80

PREP TIME

COOK TIME

SERVES

MEAL TYPE

INGREDIENTS :

INSTRUCTIONS :

NOTES :

# RECIPE : 81

PREP TIME

COOK TIME

SERVES

MEAL TYPE

INGREDIENTS :

INSTRUCTIONS :

NOTES :

# RECIPE : 82

PREP TIME

COOK TIME

SERVES

MEAL TYPE

INGREDIENTS :

INSTRUCTIONS :

NOTES :

# RECIPE : 83

PREP TIME

COOK TIME

SERVES

MEAL TYPE

INGREDIENTS :

INSTRUCTIONS :

NOTES :

# RECIPE : 84

PREP TIME

COOK TIME

SERVES

MEAL TYPE

INGREDIENTS :

INSTRUCTIONS :

NOTES :

# RECIPE : 85

PREP TIME

COOK TIME

SERVES

MEAL TYPE

INGREDIENTS :

INSTRUCTIONS :

NOTES :

# RECIPE : 86

PREP TIME

COOK TIME

SERVES

MEAL TYPE

INGREDIENTS :

INSTRUCTIONS :

NOTES :

# RECIPE : 87

PREP TIME

COOK TIME

SERVES

MEAL TYPE

INGREDIENTS :

•
•
•
•
•
•
•
•
•
•
•
•
•
•
•
•
•
•

INSTRUCTIONS :

NOTES :

# RECIPE : 88

PREP TIME

COOK TIME

SERVES

MEAL TYPE

INGREDIENTS :

INSTRUCTIONS :

NOTES :

# RECIPE : 89

PREP TIME

COOK TIME

SERVES

MEAL TYPE

INGREDIENTS :

INSTRUCTIONS :

NOTES :

# RECIPE : 90

PREP TIME

COOK TIME

SERVES

MEAL TYPE

INGREDIENTS :

INSTRUCTIONS :

NOTES :

# RECIPE : 91

PREP TIME

COOK TIME

SERVES

MEAL TYPE

INGREDIENTS :

INSTRUCTIONS :

NOTES :

# RECIPE : 92

PREP TIME

COOK TIME

SERVES

MEAL TYPE

INGREDIENTS :

INSTRUCTIONS :

NOTES :

# RECIPE : 93

PREP TIME

COOK TIME

SERVES

MEAL TYPE

INGREDIENTS :

INSTRUCTIONS :

NOTES :

# RECIPE : 94

PREP TIME

COOK TIME

SERVES

MEAL TYPE

INGREDIENTS :

INSTRUCTIONS :

NOTES :

# RECIPE : 95

PREP TIME

COOK TIME

SERVES

MEAL TYPE

INGREDIENTS :

INSTRUCTIONS :

NOTES :

# RECIPE : 96

PREP TIME

COOK TIME

SERVES

MEAL TYPE

INGREDIENTS :

INSTRUCTIONS :

NOTES :

# RECIPE : 97

PREP TIME

COOK TIME

SERVES

MEAL TYPE

INGREDIENTS :

INSTRUCTIONS :

NOTES :

# RECIPE : 98

PREP TIME

COOK TIME

SERVES

MEAL TYPE

INGREDIENTS :

- 
- 
- 
- 
- 
- 
- 
- 
- 
- 
- 
- 
- 
- 
- 
- 
- 
- 

INSTRUCTIONS :

NOTES :

# RECIPE : 99

PREP TIME

COOK TIME

SERVES

MEAL TYPE

INGREDIENTS :

INSTRUCTIONS :

NOTES :

NOTES :

NOTES :

Thank you for purchasing this book. If you enjoyed using this book, then feedback on amazon would be greatly appreciated. It would be really kind of you to take the time to write a review, which would help us immensely.

For any suggestions or questions regarding our book please contact us at the email below. To join our mailing list for our latest book releases & early bird discounts email us with Subject- 'Recipes' @
oceanicbookhub@gmail.com

Without your voice we don't exist.
Thank you for your support.

Made in United States
Troutdale, OR
12/22/2024

27175752R00062